KV-578-196

Hello, God

Copyright © 1990 Éditions du Centurion/Bayard Presse
Translation copyright © 1990 Lion Publishing plc

Published by
Lion Publishing plc
Sandy Lane West, Oxford, England
ISBN 0 7459 1959 6
Lion Publishing Corporation
1705 Hubbard Avenue, Batavia, Illinois 60510, USA
ISBN 0 7459 1959 6
Albatross Books Pty Ltd
PO Box 320, Sutherland, NSW 2232, Australia
ISBN 0 7324 0265 4

First published 1990 by Éditions du Centurion/Bayard Presse under the title
of *Images pour prier dieu*
First English edition published 1991 by Lion Publishing plc

All rights reserved

British Library CIP data and Library of Congress CIP data applied for

Printed in France
Impression et reliure : Pollina s.a., 85400 Luçon - n° 13182

My Picture Prayer Book

Hello, God

Marie-Agnès Gaudrat
Illustrations by Carmé Solé Vendrell

A LION BOOK

Oxford · Batavia · Sydney

Preface

"Where is God?" "Why can't I see him?" "Why doesn't he answer when I talk to him?" These are the simple, basic questions children always ask when they pray.

It is daunting to pray to what feels like empty space, to an invisible listener. Children need something tangible, something real to latch on to. These books are designed to provide them with pictures to focus their eyes and their thoughts. The pictures are only starting-points: like boats tied up by the water's edge, they can lead to a voyage of discovery. And to help children get started on their own prayers, each picture is accompanied by simple guidelines and a prayer.

The main theme of this book is meeting God, the basis of all prayer. There are no set prayers, no formulas, but a gentle invitation to learn how to come close to God, how to be receptive to him. As children learn to enjoy spending time with God, they will find their own ways to pray. Indeed, that is the aim of the book—to make praying as enjoyable as playing.

Prayer is about meeting God

God doesn't speak like we do.
And so, when we pray
and don't hear his voice
it's easy to talk a lot
but not listen to him.

The next three pictures
—wind, water and earth—
All say something about God.
These three pictures help us
to see how we can hear God
speaking to us.

The wind

The wind blows hard:
you can see the trees bend and sway
and the sailing boats skim over
the water,
but you never see the wind itself.
The wind blows gently:
you can feel it ruffling your hair
and see the clothes flapping
on the washing line,
but you never see the wind itself.

Dear God, I cannot see you,
but you are the breath of life.

Water

Raindrops
washing away the clouds,
trickling through the grass,
oozing into the soil,
gone.
The water
wakes the seeds
and makes the plants grow.
From water comes new life.

Dear God, I cannot hold water
in my hands and I cannot hold you,
but like the water you bring new life.

Earth

The earth soaks up
everything that falls upon it:
sun in summertime,
dead leaves in autumn,
frost, snow and rain.
It welcomes them all
and slowly, slowly,
day by day, all unseen,
it protects the tiny seeds
and feeds the plants.

Dear God, you are kind
and patient like the earth.

Prayer is about meeting God

If you want to meet someone,
you have to go to the place where they are
or ask them to come to you.
But when you want to meet God,
who is invisible to our eyes,
it's sometimes hard to know
how to find him.

The next three pictures
 —a door, a moment in time and the cross—
are to help you start to pray.

The door

A closed door
is like a wall:
you can't go through it.
If you invite someone
to come to see you,
you have to open the door
and let them in.

*Dear God, I want to be
like an open door,
ready to welcome you.*

A moment in time

How long ago?
A year? A month?
A day? An hour?
These times are past and gone.
How soon is soon?
Tomorrow? Next week? Next year?
These times are yet to come.
This very moment slipping by
is where I am
right now.

Here and now,
dear God,
I am waiting for you.

The cross

From the earth
to the heavens on high
the cross joins us to God.
From the sunrise
to the sunset,
the cross joins us
to everyone in the world.

*Feet on the ground
and head to heaven,
my arms wide open to the world,
I come to you, dear God,
reaching to your love.*

Prayer is about meeting God

We like spending time with people we love.
They help us to change,
to become better people,
to learn new things,
to grow day by day.

The next three pictures
—a wobbly toy, a pebble and a glass—
tell us something
about how praying to God can change us.

A wobbly toy

A wobbly toy is a real acrobat
who always lands the right way up.
You can knock him down
or push him over,
but back he comes.
You can hold him down on his back,
but when you let go
up he pops again.

Dear God, when you are with me,
even when life knocks me right over,
I can stand up again.

A pebble

A piece of soap
that is left in water
goes soft and melts away.
But a rock in the sea
becomes a smooth round pebble
which is nice to hold in your hand.
A little water, a little time,
and soap will melt away.
But it takes the sea
an age of time
to smooth rocks into pebbles.

Dear God, I give you my dreams
and hopes. Please shape me,
just as the pebbles
are washed smooth by the sea.

A glass

Just look into a glass
so smooth and clear.
Even a tiny drop of water
is not hidden, but can be seen.

Dear God,
make me like a glass
so that your light can shine
through me.

Prayer is about meeting God

We are not the first people
to pray and seek for God.
Before us,
and before our parents,
and before their parents,
there were other people
—men and women and children—
who believed in God
and prayed to him.

The next three pictures
—a shepherd, a path and a light—
are to look at as we talk to God.
Beside each picture are some words
which other people have used over
many, many years.

A shepherd

The Lord is my shepherd,
I shall lack nothing.
He makes me lie down
in green pastures,
he leads me beside quiet waters,
he restores my soul.

Psalm 23:1-3

The Lord is my shepherd.

The path

In you I trust,
O my God.
Do not let me be put to shame.
Show me your ways, O Lord,
teach me your paths;
guide me in your truth and teach me,
for you are my God, my helper.

From Psalm 25

Dear God,
teach me your paths
and show me your ways.

A light

The Lord is my light
and my salvation—
whom shall I fear?
The Lord is the stronghold
of my life—
of whom shall I be afraid?

Psalm 27:1

The Lord is my light.

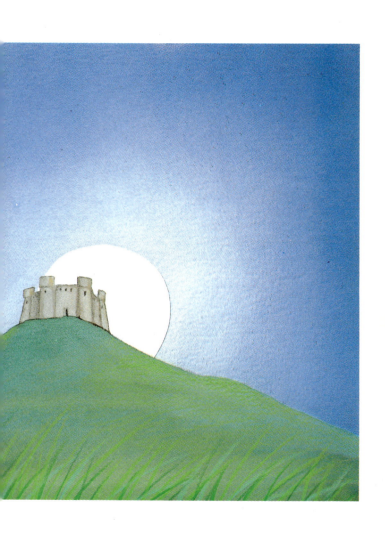

Prayer is about meeting God

Jesus, the Son of God,
became a man to show us what God is like.
He came to show us the way to God.

The next three pictures
—a father, the sun and a child—
are ones which Jesus used
to talk about God
and about the people who want to find God.

A father

When people asked Jesus
how they should pray to God,
he told them
to call God
"Father".

Luke 11:2

*Our Father God, may your name
be revered in all the world.*

The sun

Jesus told his friends,
"Love your enemies."
He reminded them that God
makes the sun rise
on bad people and good people alike
and he sends rain
on all people, too.

Matthew 5:45

Dear God,
help me to love all people
as you do.

A child

When people asked Jesus
how to be friends with God,
he said that the kingdom of heaven
belongs to people who are willing
to trust him like little children.

Matthew 19:14

Dear God, look at me:
I am a child full of life;
eager to learn about everything.

How this book works

Section 1 : Children can find it difficult to speak to a God who cannot be seen or heard. Here are three pictures to help them form a concept of what God is like: **the wind,** page 8; **water,** page 10; **earth,** page 12.

Section 2 : Just as for adults, it can be hard for a child to get into the right mood for praying. Here are three pictures to calm and focus their thoughts: **the door,** page 16; **a moment in time,** page 18; **the cross,** page 20.

Section 3 : Children often think of prayer as asking for things. To help them think of God not as a magician but as a father, here are three more pictures: **a wobbly toy,** page 24; **a pebble,** page 26; **a glass,** page 28.

Section 4 : Prayer is also a way of linking ourselves with people who have prayed in other times or in other places. Here are three pictures to help children recognize this dimension of prayer with words from three psalms from the Old Testament: **a shepherd,** page 32; **the path,** page 34; **a light,** page 36.

Section 5 : Christians recognize that Jesus came to show us what God is like. Here are three pictures to help children pray as Jesus taught: **a father,** page 40; **the sun,** page 42; **a child,** page 44.

How to use this book with children

The simplest way is to work through the book from beginning to end, stopping to look and read where the child shows interest. Or you might like to use a picture from section two to help your child start to pray.

Yet another way would be to dip into it regularly, using a familiar, relevant starting-point. For example, after a day spent playing with water or bathing, the picture of water may be particularly helpful. Or after a day spent digging, the picture of the earth may be suitable. The day before a new school year may be quite fraught, in which case the prayer about the wobbly toy may help. Gradually, children will learn to use the picture that matches their mood or the occasion.

Children who are too young to read will enjoy being read to or simply looking at the pictures. If the pictures inspire other prayers, or just quiet thought, that is fine. It is no accident that the book begins with a picture of the wind, which "blows wherever it pleases", and ends with a picture of children. They have all they need—God's Holy Spirit—to pray freely, and that is what this book invites them to do.